Fl✸wer P✸wer
punches

for cards & gifts

Jutta Feldmann

FORTE PUBLISHERS

Contents

© 2004 Forte Uitgevers, Utrecht
© 2004 for the translation by the
publisher
Original title: *Flower Power ponsen
voor kaarten en cadeautjes*

ISBN 90 5877 460 0

This is a publication from
Forte Publishers BV
P.O. Box 1394
3500 BJ Utrecht
The Netherlands

For more information about the creative
books available from Forte Uitgevers:
www.forteuitgevers.nl

Final editing: Gina Kors-Lambers,
Steenwijk, the Netherlands
Photography and digital image editing:
Fotografie Gerhard Witteveen,
Apeldoorn, the Netherlands
Cover and inner design:
BADE creatieve communicatie, Baarn,
the Netherlands
Translation: Michael Ford, TextCase,
Hilversum, the Netherlands

Preface

Flower Power. Many of you will have heard of this period and you may even have experienced it yourself. It was a short period at the end of the nineteen sixties and early nineteen seventies when people, particularly young people, freely expressed themselves. This was visible everywhere and there were flowers wherever you looked, even in the fashions of the time. But there was more to it: the skirts became shorter, the hair became longer and the shoes had platform soles. In short, it was a time of great change. Together with the exuberant lifestyle, there was also a demand for peace, which is very much alive again with the war against terrorism.

I have used punches, coloured card, beads, sequins and certain patterns to try and capture the atmosphere of this period on cards. I went back in time myself, making the cards, and I enjoyed it very much. I wish you the same.

Have fun!

Jutta

Techniques

Punching

Nowadays, there are many different types of punches available. You can divide them into groups, such as figure punches, corner punches, frame punches, border ornament punches, distance punches and many more. Since I have mainly used the above-mentioned punches in this book, I will give a short explanation of each type.

Figure punches

Figure punches come in different sizes: mini, small and medium. With these punches, you can punch different shapes, such as a flower, a heart, a butterfly, etc. There are many different shapes available. You can use the punched shapes to make very attractive cards.

Corner punches

These punches are for punching corners. They are very useful, because the sides of the punch keep the corner of the card in place.

Frame punches

With these punches, the pattern is square. If you punch a number of patterns next to each other, you will have a pretty mosaic pattern.

You can also cut out the punched mosaic patterns and stick them on the card just as you would for figure punches.

Border ornament punches

These are special punches for decorating borders. If you slide the punch along the edge of a card so that the last pattern is aligned with the first pattern, you will make an uninterrupted border pattern.

Distance punches

These punches punch to a distance of 8.5 cm in the paper and can be used just like figure punches.

In this book, I have used all the punches as figure punches. I was interested in the shapes and it does not always have to be difficult. You can do so much with them. For example, you can combine different colours or different sizes or you can stick or sew beads, sequins, buttons or adhesive stones on them. You can also make them 3D or use a gel pen to colour in the borders or you can make them bigger. You can create an embossing effect by using punched shapes which are the same colour as the card.

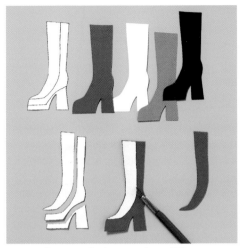

1. Draw lines on the boot and cut different coloured boots into pieces.

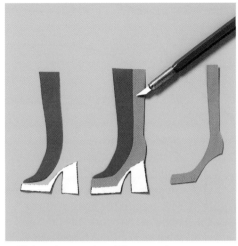

2. Make a boot using different colours.

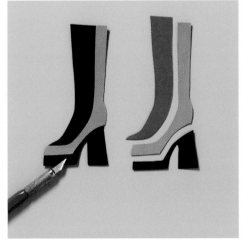

3. Make different boots.

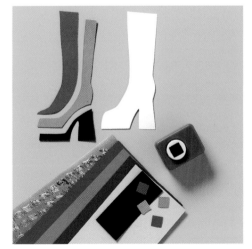

4. Decorate the boots.

Boot pattern

Tips

- Use paper which is suitable for punching. If you use figure punches, then you can also use card. The more complex the pattern of the punch, the thinner the paper must be. You can also buy punch aids, which are useful if you are using border ornament punches or frame punches. You usually punch card and if you have a punch aid, you do not have to use so much force to punch it.
- If the punched shapes do not fall out of the punch, use a pair of tweezers to remove them. Do the same if the punch gets stuck with paper in it.
- If the punches become blunt, then punch fine sandpaper or aluminium foil to sharpen them.

Boot

Copy the pattern twice and cut them out. Turn one copy over, place it on the card and use a pencil to draw around the outside. Cut it out. For a large boot, do this four times on white, black, lilac and dark violet card. Take the second copy and cut it into pieces. Place the first piece on the good side of the dark violet boot, stick it down using non-permanent adhesive tape and cut it out. Place the cut out dark violet piece on the lilac boot, stick it down using non-permanent adhesive tape and cut it out. Do the same for the sole. Cut it out, place it on the lilac boot and cut it out again. Place the lilac part on the black boot, stick it down using non-permanent adhesive tape and cut out the sole. Stick these three pieces on the white boot.

Large cards

Take an A4 card and cut off 10 cm. Fold the card double to make a large card.

Coluzzle

Place the card on the special Coluzzle cutting mat and place the template on the card. Use the special Coluzzle swivel knife to cut the lines of the template in the card. Remove the template and cut the remaining pieces loose.

Unless otherwise stated, all the patterns in this book are the correct size.

Materials

- Card and paper:
  cArt-us and Papicolor
- Circle cutter
- Ruler with a metal cutting edge
- Double-sided adhesive tape
- Glue
- Various punches
- Stickers

- Foam tape
- Paper scissors
- Tissu strips
- Ribbon
- Beads
- Sequins
- Eyelet tags
- Pricking mat

- Perforating tool
- Embellishments
- Gel pens
- Coluzzle template
- Coluzzle mat
- Coluzzle swivel knife
- Pompoms
- Adhesive stones

Flowery cards

1. Card with adhesive stones

Cut a white (Co210) square (6 x 6 cm) and
decorate it with strips, starting with a white
strip in the middle. Stick this on a Papiplus
(P184) square (6.5 x 6.5 cm) and then stick it,
standing on a point, on a white square (12 x
12 cm). Stick this on a mauve (P13) square
(12.5 x 12.5 cm) and then on a double Papiplus
(P184) card (13.5 x 13.5 cm). Use punched
shapes and adhesive stones to decorate the
white square.

2. Card with open-folded corners

Cut the back off of a white aperture card. Stick
a square which has been covered with strips
behind the opening. Stick this on a lilac (Co453)
square (13 x 13 cm) and then on an old red
(Co517) double card (14 x 14 cm). Use punched
shapes to decorate the card.

3. Large card with a heart

Copy the pattern of the heart onto white card,
cut it out and decorate it. Stick this on a
Papiplus (P184) rectangle (6.6 x 16.8 cm), then
on a dark red (Co519) rectangle (7.3 x 17.8 cm)
and finally on a white (Co210) rectangle (7.8 x
18.3 cm). Stick everything on a large mauve
(P13) double card.

4. Small card with a heart

The measurements of the small card are:
Papiplus (P184) card 3.2 x 8 cm, dark red
(Co519) card 3.7 x 8.5 cm and white (Co210)
card 4.2 x 9 cm. Stick everything on a double
card (6 x 11 cm).

Heart pattern
Card no. 3

Small heart pattern
Card no. 4

Flower pattern
Card no. 5

5. Card with a large flower

Cut a white (Co210) square (13 x 13
cm). Use a pencil to draw a thin line 6.5 cm
from the top. Stick the strips on the white
square, starting in the middle. Cut a dark red
(Co519) strip (1 x 13 cm) and stick it on the ends
of the strips. Stick everything on a dark red
square (13.5 x 13.5 cm) and then on a double
lilac (Co453) card (14 x 14 cm). Use punched
shapes to decorate the white part of the card.
Copy the pattern of the large flower onto

Papiplus (P184)
card and cut it out. Use
punched shapes to decorate it and
use foam tape to stick it on the middle of
the strip.

A bit hip

All the cards and all the large squares are the same size. The double cards measure 11 x 11 cm. The small square measures 10 x 10 cm.

1. Card with a butterfly
Stick squares on a dark violet (P46) square (10 x 10 cm) in the following order: violet (Co425 - 5.2 x 5.2 cm), mint (Co331 - 5 x 5 cm), light blue (Co391 - 4.5 x 4.5 cm) and dark violet (P46 - 4 x 4 cm). Use different coloured punched shapes to decorate the card

and sew a bead in the middle of the shapes. Stick black dots between the punched shapes and stick the butterfly in the middle of the card.

2. Card with hearts
You need four hearts in different colours and of different sizes. Copy two hearts onto card using the find-cut template. Copy the heart pattern once and punch the smallest heart. Use the gel pen to draw around the outside edge of the

Heart pattern
Card no. 2

hearts and stick them on top of each other. Stick the punched shapes with a white dot in the middle on the turquoise (P32) square around the heart. Prick a hole in every leaf and sew beads on them. Stick small dots between the punched shapes.

3. Card with a pink flower

Copy the flower pattern onto pink card (P15) and cut it out. Use the gel pen to draw around

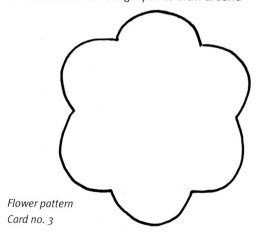

Flower pattern
Card no. 3

the outside edge of the flower and decorate it as shown in the photograph. Stick it on a turquoise (P32) square (10 x 10 cm). Decorate the card as described for the card with a butterfly.

4. Lilac card with a flower

Use the metal template to copy the flower onto mauve card (P13) and cut it out. Use the gel pen to draw around the outside edge. Stick

a punched shape with a dot in the middle of the flower. Stick it on a dark violet (P46) square (4 x 4 cm) and stick that on a lilac (Co453) square (4.5 x 4.5 cm), a lavender (Co487) square (5 x 5 cm) and a dark violet (P46) square (10 x 10 cm). Stick different coloured, punched shapes around it and decorate the card as described for card 2.

1.

2.

3.

4.

Flower Power

What you need
Card • Letter stickers: silver • Sequins in a tube:
lilac • Beads: turquoise, red and dark violet
• Buttons: mix • Frame punch: flower • Distance
punch: small hole • Corner punch: dove • Figure
punches: daisy (large and small) • Mini punch:
clover • Letter beads • Eyelet tags • Make Me
hand punch: Ø 1/16 inch • Transparent sheet
• Glitter gel pen: purple • Embroidery silk
• Perforating tool and mat • Cardstock stickers
• K & Company Juliana embossed stickers
• Tissu strips (5 mm): lilac/purple mix and
blue mix • Tissu strips (3 mm): lilac/purple mix

1. Elongated Flower Power card
Cut a white rectangle (7.3 x 18 cm). Copy the
pricking pattern, stick it on the white rectangle
and prick the pattern. Prick an extra hole in the
middle of each loop to sew beads onto the card.
Use double-sided adhesive tape to stick the
letter beads on the punched shapes. Stick the
white rectangle on a light blue (C0391) rectangle
(7.8 x 18.5 cm) and a turquoise (P32) rectangle
(8.3 x 19 cm). Stick everything on a large, dark
violet (P46) double card.

2. Flower Power
Cut a white (P190) Papiplus square (12.5 x
12.5 cm), a mint (C0331)
square (13 x 13 cm) and a
light blue (C0391) square
(13.5 x 13.5 cm). Stick
them on a dark violet (P46)
double card (14.7 x 14.7
cm). Stick stickers and punched shapes on the
white square as shown in the photograph. Use
foam tape to stick the butterfly on the letter "O".

3. Card with a flower
Cut a rectangle (2.5 x 9 cm) out of a transparent
sheet and stick different coloured strips of
different sizes on it. Stick a thin stem made from
spring green (C0305) card behind the strips.
Use the metal template to copy the flower onto
light blue (C0391) card, cut it out and stick it on
the end of the stem. Use two punched shapes
to decorate the flower and stick them on so
that one is slightly at an angle compared to the
other. You can use double-sided adhesive tape
to stick the vase on the card where the widest
strips are. Use a small amount of glue to stick
the flower on the card. Punch flowers out of
dark violet (P46) card and lilac (C0453) card,
rotate them so that they are at a slight angle
compared to each other and stick them on top
of each other. Use double-sided adhesive tape

Pricking pattern for card no. 1: increase in size by 110%

to stick the letter beads between the punched shapes. Stick this decorated, white rectangle (7 x 17.8 cm) on light blue (C0391) card (7.5 x 18.3 cm) and then on turquoise (P32) card (8 x 18.8 cm). Stick everything on a dark violet double (P46) card.

4. Card with a green flower

Copy the pattern and use non-permanent tape to stick it on a white (C0210) square (11 x 11 cm). Prick the pattern and cut it out around the outside. Remove the pattern. Turn the card over and prick a hole in the middle of each loop. Turn the white square over again and use the holes in the loops to sew red beads on the card. Stick stickers in the middle of the white square. Sew a button in each corner and in the middle of the flower. Prick

Pricking pattern for card no. 4: increase in size by 110%

Peace sign pattern for card no. 5: increase in size by 110%

holes before sewing the button in place, because this will stop the thread from being visible through the white card later. Stick the decorated square on a spring green (C0305) square (11.5 x 11.5 cm), a light blue (C0391) square (12 x 12 cm) and a turquoise (P32) square (12.5 x 12.5 cm). Stick everything on a dark violet (P46) card (14.7 x 14.7 cm).

5. Card with the peace sign

Make four copies of the embroidery pattern, cut them out and use non-permanent adhesive tape to stick them in the four corners of a white square (12.7 x 12.7 cm). Place it on a pricking mat and prick the pattern. Use adhesive tape to stick down the start and end of the embroidery silk at the rear of the card. Insert the needle into hole 1 from the back to the front and then insert the needle in hole 9 from the front to the back. Insert the needle into hole 10 from the back to the front and then into hole 2 from the front to the back. Once you have finished the embroidery, rub all the holes closed on the back of the card. Stick two

Pricking pattern
for card no. 5

sequins in the middle of every embroidered pattern. Prick a hole and sew a bead on every sequin. The sequin may come loose after pricking the hole, but that is not too serious, because the hole will tell you where the sequin should be. Copy the pattern of the peace sign onto lilac (C0453) card, cut it out and use a gel pen to draw around the outside edges. Stick it on dark violet (P46) card and cut it out. Use letter stickers to write the word "Peace". Stick a small dove inside the peace sign. Stick the peace sign on the white card. Stick punched flowers on the card which are slightly rotated compared to each other. Stick the decorated square card on a light blue (C0391) square (13.2 x 13.2 cm) and then on a turquoise (P32) square (13.7 x 13.7 cm). Stick everything on a dark violet (P46) double card (14.7 x 14.7 cm).

6. Earth laughs

Cut a white (C0210) square (12.5 x 12.5 cm), a spring green (C0305) square (13 x 13 cm) and a turquoise (P32) square (13.5 x 13.5 cm). Stick them on a dark violet (P46) double card (14.7 x 14.7 cm). Stick stickers and punched shapes on the white square as shown in the photograph.

Peace

What you need
Card • Figure punches: flower and Carla Craft
flower • Sequins: gold and flower • Glitter
gel pens: purple and burgundy • Beads: red,
gold and orange • Perforating tool and mat
• Embroidery silk • Find-cut template: heart

1. Mauve card with a large heart

Make a mauve (P13) double card (13.5 x 13.5 cm).
Place the fold facing towards you and cut 0.5 cm
off of the front (fold the card open first). Cut an
orange (C0545) rectangle (10 x 13.5 cm) and
fold it 5 cm from the edge to make a double
card (5 x 13.5 cm).
Decorate the front of the orange card according
to the instructions for card no. 4. Once you have
finished, stick the rear of the orange card to the
rear of the mauve card. Use the metal template
to copy the large heart onto orange (C0545)

card and cut it out. Stick it on the front of the
card and decorate it as described for card no. 4.
Decorate the inside with a piece of card which
is 0.5 cm smaller than the front of the card. Use
double-sided adhesive tape to stick this card
in place.

2. Flowers

This card is made according to the instructions
for card no. 4. The orange rectangle measures
9.2 x 20.3 cm. Stick this on a large grass green
card.

3. Mauve card with a large flower

Cut an orange (C0545) square (13 x 13 cm) and
use it to make a 3 cm wide frame. Decorate
the frame as shown in the photograph (see card
no. 4 for instructions). Stick it on a lemon yellow
(P09) square (13.5 x 13.5 cm) and then on a
mauve (P13) double card (14.7 x 14.7 cm).
Copy the pattern of the flower onto orange and
yellow card, cut them out and use a gel pen to
draw around the outside edges. Stick the
orange flower at an angle on the yellow flower.
Stick a punched shape on it and use a bead to
stick a sequin in the middle. Stick this on an
orange square (6.4 x 6.4 cm) and then stick it
in the middle of the frame.

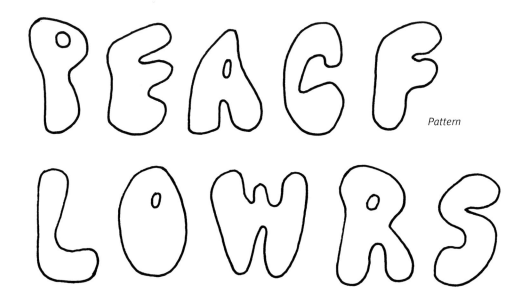

Pattern

4. Peace card

Cut an orange (Co545) square (13 x 13 cm). Stick the flower sequins on the punched shapes, pushing them down firmly. Copy the letters onto different coloured card, cut them out and use the gel pen to draw around the outside edges. Stick the letters together with each letter slightly overlapping the one next to it as shown in the photograph. Place the punched shapes and the sequins in the correct positions before using glue to stick them in place. Prick through the holes in the sequins. The sequin may come loose, but that is not a problem, because the hole in the card will tell you where the sequin should be. Sew red and gold beads onto the sequins. Use glue to stick the word on the orange card before sticking it on a grass green (P07) double card (13.5 x 13.5 cm). Decide where you wish to have the word "Peace" before sticking it on the card.

5. Orange card with three hearts

This card is made according to the instructions given for card 1. Take a large orange (Co545) double card and place it with the fold facing towards you. Fold it open and cut 0.5 cm off. Cut a mauve (P13) rectangle (9 x 20.8 cm) and fold it 4.5 cm from the edge. Follow the instructions given for card 2. Use the small heart from the template.

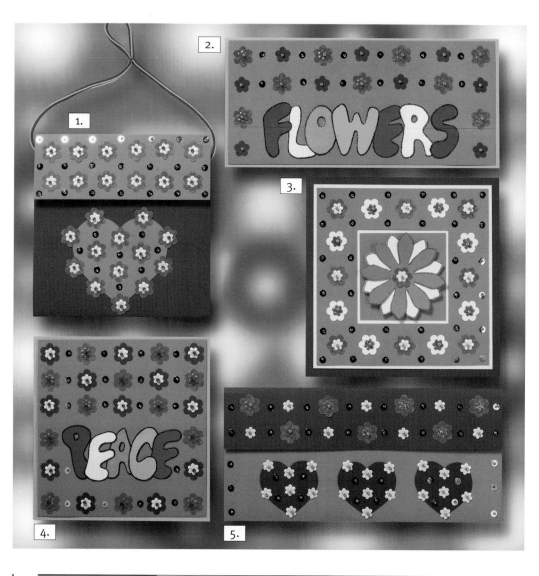

1.

2.

3.

4.

5.

Red cards

What you need

Card • Find-cut template • Figure punches:
daisy (large and small) • Frame punch: flowers
• Distance punch: small hole • Photo corner
punch • Pompoms: orange and red • Home punch
• Orange ribbon • Beads: orange • Foam tape
• Perforating tool and mat • Ornare vellum stencil:
PR 0561 • Circle cutter

1. Red card with a wreath of flowers

Place the stencil on red card, use a pencil to draw
around the outside and cut it out. Use a circle
cutter to cut the circle out of the middle. Place
the stencil exactly on top, use two
pins to keep it in place and prick
the pattern on the good side of
the card. Turn the card over
and prick some extra holes
to sew beads on the card as
shown in the photograph.
Stick punched flowers
on the good side of
the card between
the pricked
pattern. Stick
a yellow circle
behind the opening
which is slightly

Extra hole

*Pricking pattern
for card no. 1*

bigger than the circle cut out in the middle. Stick
the rest of the punched shapes on the card as
shown in the photograph. Stick a large daisy in
the middle of the yellow circle. Stick this on an
orange (Co545) square (13 x 13 cm) and then on
a golden yellow (Co247) square (13.5 x 13.5 cm).
Stick everything on an old red (Co517) card (14.7 x
14.7 cm). Use punched shapes to decorate the
corners of the orange card.

2. Red card with three hearts inside each other

Use the find-cut template to copy the hearts
onto card. Cut them out and stick them on top
of each other. Decorate the orange and red
hearts with dots and punched shapes. Stick a

large daisy in the middle of the yellow heart. Stick this on a golden yellow (Co247) square (12.5 x 12.5 cm) and then on an orange (Co545) square (13 x 13 cm). Stick everything on an old red (Co517) double card (14.7 x 14.7 cm). Decorate the yellow card with pompoms and punched shapes as shown in the photograph.

3. Horizontal card with two hearts

Use the template to copy the medium-sized heart twice onto old red (Co517) card and cut them out. Decorate them and stick them on a golden yellow (Co247) rectangle (7.5 x 19 cm). Use small punched shapes to decorate them as shown in the photograph and stick them on an orange (Co545) rectangle (8 x 19.5 cm) and then on a large, old red (Co517) double card.

4. Orange card with a heart in the middle

Cut three old red (Co517) squares (13 x 13 cm, 11 x 11 cm and 6.3 x 6.3 cm), a golden yellow

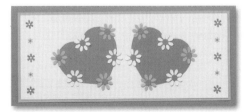

(Co247) square (11.5 x 11.5 cm) and an orange (Co545) square (9.5 x 9.5 cm). Stick the squares on top of each other on an orange double card (13.5 x 13.5 cm).

Use the template to copy the small and the medium-sized hearts, cut them out and stick them on top of each other. Stick a punched shape in the middle and stick this in the middle of the red square.

Use foam tape to stick punched shapes on the orange border. Wind an orange ribbon with beads on the end around the card.

5. Elongated card with two hearts

Use the template to copy the large heart onto old red (Co517) card and golden yellow card and cut them out. Use punched shapes to decorate them as shown in the photograph and stick them on an orange (Co545) rectangle (8 x 20 cm). Decorate this with small flowers before sticking it on a golden yellow rectangle (8.5 x 20.5 cm) and an old red (Co517) double card.

Indian cloths

All the cards have the same dimensions
(see Techniques).

What you need

Card• *Figure punches: daisy (large and small)*
• Corner punch: dove • Frame punch: flowers and
butterfly • Border ornament punch: heart and
dove • Distance punch: small hole • Hole punch
• Make Me hand punch: Ø 1/16 inch • Eyelet tags

1. Elongated lavender card with small butterflies

The instructions for this card are the same as
those for card no. 3. Cut a dark violet (P46)
rectangle (8.3 x 19.2 cm) and a turquoise (P32)
rectangle (7.9 x 18.8 cm) and stick them on
a lavender (C0487) double card. Decorate a
grass green (P07) rectangle (7.5 x 18.4 cm)
with punched shapes and eyelet tags before
sticking it on the card.

2. Light blue card with four doves

The instructions for this
card are the same as
those for card no. 3.
Cut a pine green (P45)
rectangle (8 x 18.9 cm) and
a spring green (C0305)
rectangle (7.5 x 18.4 cm)
and stick them on a large,
light blue (C0391) double
card. Cut two mint (C0331) rectangles (7 x
8.7 cm) and decorate them with card and
paper eyelet tags and punched shapes before
sticking them on the card.

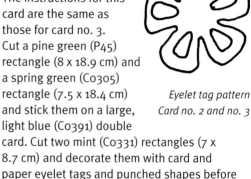

Eyelet tag pattern
Card no. 2 and no. 3

3. Elongated aqua blue card with doves

Cut a turquoise (P32) rectangle (8 x 18.8 cm) and
a light blue (C0391) rectangle (7.5 x 18.3 cm) and
stick them on a large, aqua blue (C0427) double
card. Punch six large flowers, cut them in half
and decorate them with punched leaves. Use
a small amount of glue to stick them on a light
blue (P42) rectangle (7 x 17.8 cm), starting in the
corners. Use punched shapes to decorate the
rectangle as shown in the photograph. Copy the
pattern, cut it out and place it on the back of light
blue card. Use a pencil to draw around the inside

1.

2.

3.

4.

and outside of the pattern. Cut out the middle pieces first before cutting out the pattern. Also do this with Papiplus paper (P187), but only cut around the circumference. Stick the patterns on top of each other on the good side of the card. Stick a white dot in the middle before sticking them on the light blue rectangle. Do the same for the eyelet tags. Stick the punched doves on them before sticking them on the card.

4. Elongated lilac card

The instructions for this card are the same as those for card no. 3. Cut a mauve (P13) rectangle (8.3 x 19.3 cm) and an orange (Co545) rectangle (7.9 x 18.9 cm) and stick them on a lilac (Co487) double card. Decorate a salmon (Co482) rectangle (7.5 x 18.5 cm) with punched shapes and eyelet tags before sticking it on the card.

Shopping

Hat pattern
Card no. 1

1. Card with a hat

Copy the pattern of the hat onto
white (C0210) card, dark violet
card (P46) and violet card
(C0425). Cut them out and
follow the instructions given
in Techniques. Decorate the
hat with sequins and use glue
to stick Funny Fibre between
the violet and the dark violet
cards. Decorate a pink (C0481)
rectangle (7.5 x 18 cm) with
squares (the black squares
measure 1.1 x 1.1 cm, but
you can also use a
punch), a black hat
stand, stickers and
the hat as shown in
the photograph. Stick this on a light blue
(C0391) rectangle (8 x 18.5 cm), a dark violet
rectangle (8.5 x 19 cm) and a
large lilac (C0453) double card.

Hat stand pattern
Card no. 1

2. Card with small boots

Copy the pattern three times
onto white, black and coloured
card for each boot. Make the
boots as described in
Techniques. Decorate the boots
with sequins, beads, buttons,
Funny Fibres and adhesive
stones. Use a small
amount of glue to first
stick the sequins and
buttons in the correct
position, then prick a
hole and sew a bead

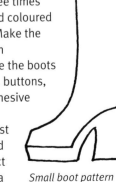

Small boot pattern
Card no. 2

on them. Use a small piece of double-sided adhesive tape to stick one end of the Funny Fibre to the back of the card, wind it three or four times around the boot and use adhesive tape to stick the other end to the back of the card. Cut an orange (Co545) rectangle (8.5 x 19.2 cm) and an old red (Co517) rectangle (8 x 18.7 cm) and stick them on a large mauve (P13) card. Stick the small boots and a narrow black strip (1 x 7.5 cm) (with a sticker on it) on a mint (Co331) rectangle (7.5 x 18.2 cm) before sticking it on the card.

3. Card with bags

Copy the pattern onto spring green (Co305) card, orange (Co545) card and dark violet (P46) card. Cut them out and use a gel pen to draw around the outside edges. Prick two holes just below the line of the gel pen. Thread beads onto metal thread to make the handle of the bag. Slide the ends of the

Bag pattern
Card no. 3

thread through the holes from the front to the back, wind it around once and pull it tight. Decorate the bags with beads, buttons and sequins. For the green bag, use beads to attach the sequins. Prick holes for beads between the sequins. Cut a red oval and stick stickers on it. Stick the oval and the bags on a soft pink (Co480) rectangle (7.5 x 18 cm). Use adhesive tape to stick a black strip (0.5 x 18 cm) with a border sticker at the bottom of the soft pink rectangle. Stick this on a mauve (P13) rectangle (8 x 18.5 cm), then on an old red (Co517) rectangle (8.5 x 19 cm) and finally on a large, orange double card.

4. Card with a boot

The instructions for making the boot are given in Techniques. Cut a black strip (3 x 7 cm) and stick it at the top of a light blue (Co391) rectangle (7 x 17.8 cm). Punch or cut some squares (1.1 x 1.1 cm), stick letters on them to form the word "Gift" and use them to decorate the black strip. Stick the boot, which you have decorated with butterflies, on the card as shown in the photograph. Stick the decorated rectangle on a mauve (P13) rectangle, then on an orange (Co545) rectangle (8 x 18.8 cm) and finally on an old red (Co517) double card.

Oh man

All the large cards have the same dimensions (see Techniques).

What you need
Card • Tissu strips: yellow mix (3 mm) • Eyelet tags • Figure punch: flower and small flower • Distance punch: small hole • Make Me hand punch: Ø 1/16 inch • Coluzzle cutting mat, swivel knife and circle template • Hole punch

1. Small cards

All the small double cards measure 6 x 11 cm. On the small cards, the layers measure 3.7 x 8.1 cm, 4.2 x 8.6 cm and 4.7 x 9.1 cm. To make this card, look at the photographs and read the instructions given for cards 3, 4 and 5.

2. Bow in a retro style

Small tie pattern Card no. 1

Place the card, with the template on top, on the special Coluzzle cutting mat and use the special Coluzzle swivel knife to cut the inner two lines of the template. Remove the template and cut the remaining pieces loose.

Copy the pattern of the bow onto cream (C0241) card and cut it out. Decorate it with Coluzzle rings and dots as shown in the photograph. Cut a strip (1.5 x 16.5 cm) which is the same colour as the bow. Stick the bow on this strip and stick this on a mango (P40) rectangle (6.2 x 16.5 cm), a cream (C0241) rectangle (6.7 x 17 cm), a golden yellow (C0247) rectangle (7.2 x 17.5 cm) and an orange (C0454) rectangle (8.2 x 18.5 cm). Stick this on a large terracotta (C0549) card.

3. Tie with large flowers

Copy the circumference of the flower eyelet tag onto orange (C0454) card, terracotta (C0549) card and lemon (P09) card. Cut them out and decorate them with a punched shape before sticking them on the tie. Cut the excess card away. Stick the tie on a mango (P40) rectangle (6.2 x 16.4 cm), a lemon (P09) rectangle (6.7 x 16.9 cm), a terracotta (C0549) rectangle (6.2 x 17.4 cm) and an orange (C0454) rectangle (8.2 x 18.4 cm). Stick everything on a large mango (P40) card.

4. Tie with strips

Copy the pattern of the tie. Decorate it with small yellow and orange strips and 1 cm wide strips of terracotta (C0549) paper, starting at the bottom with a yellow strip. Always cut the strips slightly

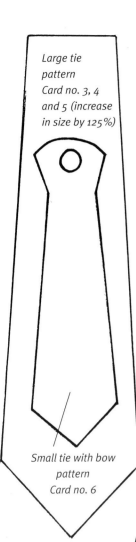

Large tie pattern Card no. 3, 4 and 5 (increase in size by 125%)

Small tie with bow pattern Card no. 6

Bow pattern Card no. 2

Small flower pattern Card no. 1, 5 and 6

longer than they need to be. Cut the excess paper off later. Stick the decorated tie on a mango (P40) rectangle (6.2 x 16.5 cm), an orange (C0545) rectangle (6.6 x 16.9 cm), a terracotta (C0549) rectangle (7.1 x 17.4 cm) and a lemon (P09) rectangle (8.1 x 18.4 cm). Stick everything on a cream (C0241) double card.

5. Tie with small flowers

Decorate a cream (C0241) tie with flowers as shown in the photograph. Stick the tie on a mango (P40) rectangle (6.5 x 16.4 cm), a golden yellow (C0247) rectangle (7 x 16.9 cm), a terracotta (C0549) rectangle (7.5 x 17.4 cm) and a cream (C0241) rectangle (8 x 17.9 cm). Stick everything on an orange (C0545) double card.

6. A bunch of ties

Copy the pattern onto different coloured card. Stick punched shapes and dots on the ties as shown in the photograph.

Many thanks to Kars & Co B.V. in Ochten, the Netherlands, and Papicolor International B.V. in Utrecht, the Netherlands, for providing the materials. Shopkeepers can order the materials from the companies above.

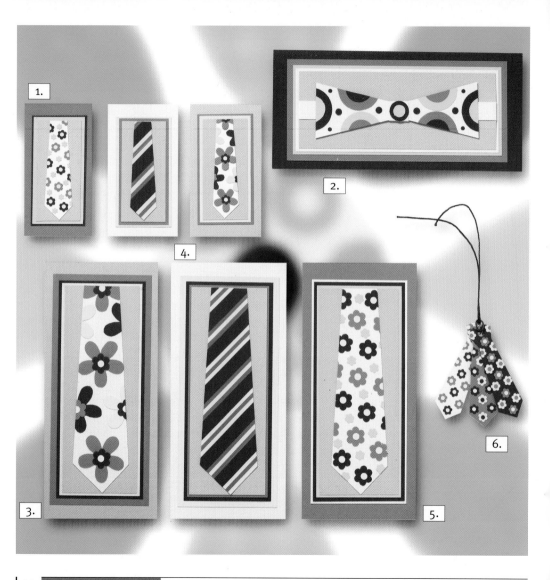

1.

2.

4.

3.

5.

6.